Ameera Abdelgawad is a holistic healing practitioner, a homeopath and a Reiki master who originally studied business administration but later followed her passion studying and practicing holistic healing, also a scholar of Sufism. She was fond of writing at a young age but has pursued her calling again since 2014. Ameera's love for mystic poetry and literature has left a print on her that comes out as creative writing in poetic expression.

Dedication

To God, who created the word and the word carries his secrets. To the One; the Only, whose creation is in unity. May these words act in bringing hearts and souls together.

Ameera Abdelgawad

SOFIA

AUSTIN MACAULEY PUBLISHERS™
LONDON • CAMBRIDGE • NEW YORK • SHARJAH

Copyright © Ameera Abdelgawad 2024

The right of Ameera Abdelgawad to be identified as author of this work has been asserted by the author in accordance with Federal Law No. (7) of UAE, Year 2002, Concerning Copyrights and Neighboring Rights.

All rights reserved. No part of this publication may be reproduced, stored in a retrieval system, or transmitted in any form or by any means, electronic, mechanical, photocopying, recording, or otherwise, without the prior permission of the publishers.

Any person who commits any unauthorized act in relation to this publication may be liable to legal prosecution and civil claims for damages.

The age group that matches the content of the books has been classified according to the age classification system issued by the Ministry of Culture and Youth.

ISBN – 9789948781929 – (Paperback)
ISBN – 9789948781936 – (E-Book)

Application Number: MC-10-01-2657911
Age Classification: E

Printer Name: iPrint Global Ltd
Printer Address: Witchford, England

First Published 2024
AUSTIN MACAULEY PUBLISHERS FZE
Sharjah Publishing City
P.O Box [519201]
Sharjah, UAE
www.austinmacauley.ae
+971 655 95 202

Acknowledgement

My mother, who carried me to life and taught me how to love, my late father, who strived I learn about it. My family, you give utmost meaning to my world. My mentors; everyone who guided me through it, you are my steppingstones to the truth. My soul tribe, I feel home with you. You, the one who reads and feels the words are yours, they are, because in reality, we are one.

To all the mornings we missed
I send solace
To all the nights past us
I send remorse
To the unfinished conversations
Unexpressed love
and lonely times we bared
I send consolation
May we find peace
In our separation

~ Soul Solace

They asked me who is she
I said you mean to question
who could she be
Sofia is the one
Who dared to love whole heartedly
Interpreted messages beyond physical reality
She is that part of your soul that longs to become whole
She is the gasp, the whisper, the look
That in the absence of the mind
Your heart took
She is the silence among your words
Your deepest desire to reach realms beyond this world
Sofia is You and I and this moment in time
All the meanings you can match her with She is

~ Sofia

Running away from what I cannot escape
Hiding from what I cannot hide
Your love has burnt me
Flesh and blood
Afraid I am
That the awes and the flames
Have nailed my soul
And missed my skin

~ Burnt

The Arabs say
A man's longing for his love
Is longing for part of his soul
A woman's longing is for her whole
I wonder who longs more the part or the whole

~ A Wonder

An ancient oath my soul endured
Carrying the truth for life to unfold
I search and search an empty cup
Looking out for YOU to quench my thirst
I seek and seek and I all find
Are traces of this old vicinity
So let bare this archaic love
In a world who barley recalls its phases
Or let me die trying to reach
The sacredness of its ancient places
I walk and walk and I can't hide
Evidence of YOU is all I find

~ The Oath

The mind says grow
The heart says NO
The soul whispers "Surrender"
When will you learn that
In order to grow you'll have
To be strong but as well tender
Easy on your heart
Your companion in this land
And also there under

~ Not All Battles Are on a Battlefield

Let them judge
We'll leave
And carry not
But this love

~ Let Them Judge

Let's float, let's flow
Let's dwell
Let's sprinkle spells
Let's submerge in eternal light
Let's be insane and rise
In the absence of the mind
Let's bloom
Let's blossom
Let's flourish
In the rays of the sun
Let's fall in the nothingness that we are
Let's race the stairs up the ladders of the skies
Let's vanish in this world and appear in another realm
Let's bath in moonlight
And shed our shells
Let's grow the seeds of a love so true
Let's surrender to who we are

~ Alive

I'm a visitor of word's wonderland
Like Alice in her wonderland
Grateful to the lord for watering my land
Wondering how much a soul withstands
Of tasting a drop dripping of YOUR hand

~ Heaven in Words

If time does heal
Then tell me why
My heart is still purging
How many lives do I need to be purified
Do I have to get crucified
My torture is not any less
Ask me not what a body withstands
There is no greater pain than one banished from their land
Ask me not what a soul can deny
When it's forced to live in exile
Ask me not to be strong and endure
My years are passing with no cure
Ask me not what I wish to be
I stopped searching for lost parts of me
If time does heal
Then why am I not back to me

~ Lost in Her Pain

I would choose you a hundred times
I'd scream out loud to the world you're mine
I'd walk with you side by side
I'd climb out mountains and dig down mines
I'd fetch you stars every night
cover you up with moonlight
and wake you up by sunrise
I'd Stretch your nights till day light
And draw them by my lines
I'd take your breath away
And make you regret you did not stay
I'd listen to your silence before your words
I'd share my soul with you if I may
I'd be your love to eternity
I am the one made for thee

~ For You I Would

When the bird flees the cage
It first wonders
But then roams the winds of change
And witness wonders

~ On Change

Like the river flowing towards the ocean
My heart flows your way
Not knowing where else to belong
Not knowing if it's the river longing
Or the ocean calling
Just flowing

~ Flowing

Watch your tides
They have more to show you in mere stillness
In your solitude
You will discover
More about your being than you seldomly utter
Dig, there is more to uncover
You will learn to gaze deeper than any looks
You will grasp knowledge with no books
You will shed layers off yourself
You will fly lighter than feathers
And dive deeper than ever
Watch your tides
They come and go
Only to reveal you

~ On Self Discovery

Flow like a leaf in the wind
or wood on water
Do they have a will of their own
Flow like there is no tomorrow
Or there has been no yesterday
Know that the ONE shall pave your way
By His will you shall not stray
Flow and you shall glow
For HIS light will find you
In the most explicit way

~ Faith

The sound of the wind
Speaks to us of HIS greatness
The chill of our longing and weakness
Be silent and listen

~ Silent and Listen Are of the Same Letters

Had you known in your cocoon
Your short-lived life
Growing your wings, yearning for freedom
Daring to fly
Had you known they were made to chase the light
Oh poor Butterfly
How fragile
Burning in flames
Had you known what lights your path
Can also catch on fire
Don't get lost in your desire

~ Fragile

She met him
And everything changed

~ It Takes a Moment to Fall in Love

Let me share some of the secrets
Of her tale
She kept on loving
despite the distance,
the bitterness, the pain
Her love was an untamed hurricane
She followed the wind
To a destined dead end
She passed the horrors
Of her own sorrows
Like a wildflower in the rain
With faith her love is not in vain
She still believed in her hurricane

~ Hurricane Called 'Love'

My heart is wrapped and tangled
Around your name
Making knots of an eternal bond
Every time I call for you
How can I escape you then
When everywhere I turn
It's only you I see

~ *I Have Found God*

I asked her to talk to the moon
On my behalf
For so long I have been speechless
Now I can't take it back
I asked her to speak of my longing and belonging
Tell him what no more words can tell
Ask him mercy for this shattered heart
Beg "enough of these worlds apart"
Plea for an eternal union
For the moon in its entirety
Cry out loud "our souls are thirsty"

~ Reaching Out

A volcano that fails to erupt
Settles in silence
Yet the flames of lava can burn millions
Years of yearning
Miles of fire
Fail in comparison to a hearts desire
Traveling ashes burnt by the lashes of a true admirer
Masses of magma are magnets to the explosions of a soulful heart
Oh worshiper had you known
From the start
How you'd endure all this fire

~ Fire Is a Love Element

In the realm of Heavens
We meet
Unlike me
I ask, you answer
I turn tables "There"
You "Here"
Like Two sides of the coin
but one in truth
Is there any more of me that is not you
Or anymore of You that is not me
Any description
Is an inadequate under estimation
Unity is fair enough

~ Elsewhere Encounters

Lost, wounded, waiting
What more can I tell of my heart without you
How can I stand to lose you after I found you
I've lived when you were with me
And died when you departed
What do I tell my heart of you
He's left me broken hearted?
How can I possibly forgive you
I've solely dwelled on suffering
How could I possibly not
The love of my life is parting
Solace to my heart and yours
Again and again
May the years be kinder to us
than our own hearts

~ On Heart Break

Like the calm above the storm
Your love is inflicted on my heart
From an outrageous thunder
I'm split apart
An outlander I am
One in spirit
and one at heart

~ *Outlander*

For them love is a four-letter word
For me
the four-letter word
Is your name
And if love fails them
They blame on love
For me
my heart is to blame

~ I'll Take the Blame

I feel sorry for you sun
You shine unnoticed until you're gone
Burning in blazes night and day
To warm cold bodies and ruthless hearts
Sending your light to everyone
Even the moon dims if you part
You rise in grace and set in silence
Wishing dull minds to find stillness in the darkness beyond long days
I'm so sorry for you sun
You stand out in the vast sky
All rotating around you
What nurtures their hopes
You're so strong they say
I see it in your eyes sun 'They lie'
I'm so sorry for you sun
Stand for yourself before you die
Make them start to question why
Did we take her love for granted
Rise in Heaven sun and fly

~ Taken for Granted

I want to swim the eternal silver rays of the moon to the isles of your light
I want to step on the marks of your footsteps along my path
I want to be all you
If there is any left of me that isn't prior to your encounter
I'll plead to it come true
I want to leave my shadows behind
Strip my fake skin and rise
Seek the naked truth and find
All the roads to paradise
So if you love me
My all-time full moon
Give me a sign

~ A Sign

The constellations were witnesses of my solitude
The shooting stars burnt from my flames
The waves crashes were rebelling my silence
Nature was conspiring against me
To kneel in prayer
It has been long since I confessed

~ Conspiracy

All the days I've witnessed your absence
Or the nights sleepless in your presence
The hollow steeping in my heart wishing you by my side
The nod bonding us with chords of light
The longing unbarred
The love we shared
The words with more cherished meanings
The cautious steps, the gentle withdrawal
The Unfading feelings
Where do I seek you now I'm forsaken
Where do I go with this heart shaken
Why don't I lose hope
Every time you leave me broken
Why does my heart have to bear your tides
Why don't I get the lesson that by broken wings
I must let you go
For I cannot allow my all to you

~ Connection

No need No greed
No fear of the unseen
Just love for the worlds beyond
Surpassing the aches we live here

~ Finding Peace

Ripples of memories
Moments of quite adoration
Pleads of a heart seeking salvation
A heart beat by YOU
beat by beat no hesitation
Blink by blink
An Eternal desire
To extinguish this blazing fire
Who am I
An everlasting contemplation
Oh dear lord
Keep this sunrise a little more
Let my eyes dwell like never before
Let my soul swim in a sea of stillness
Let my heart rest in the warmth of my breath
Let me pour down love on a hundred notes
Let me stare at silhouettes
And dance to the sensation
Let me live forever young
By this mystical imagination
Let me die for YOU
In utter prostration

~ The Heart Rhymes Prayers

Like melting snow
I need to wash myself off you
To escape my reality
To change form
Perhaps then from you I'll flee

~ Escape

I used to fear the truth
But now the truth I strive
I used to hide my feelings
And master the disguise
I now no longer bear
But look it in the eye
And beg for mercy for those
Who are still wearing their lies

I used to fear myself
For the passion I hold inside
I used to slow down
walk next to others side by side
I now no longer can
But leap in faith and pride
And plea in compassion
For those I left behind

I used to fear the unknown
And settle for what's shown
Until the fake skin killed me
There's a secret temptation
Of all that is true

In spite the suffering the ugliness
and the pain
There is magic that fulfils me

~ On Growth

Blind my eyes
The light in my heart is divine

~

A sky of pink and blue
A soul longing for you
The sun and the moon both present
Gazing at each other
Separate but one in essence
How in a vast universe they manifest
As two distant beauties at rest
Where in reality, they're drawn
Like magnet to each other
All they wish to own
A present moment of perfection
When they merge as one creation
In the marvellousness of their separation
They so long to become one

~ One Moon, One Sun

In the matters of the heart
Ask not who have not known
Loss, longing or grief
Ask not those who murmur knowledge
Or intellect, ask best those who believe
Ask the ones whose silence in volumes speak
In the matters of the heart
True ones know no mischief
For in Their journey dwell hidden treasures
As here & there, their wisdom steeps
It's a matter of belief

~ *Matters of the Heart*

My heart burns
Like a slim cigarette
Slowly and surely
The fumes of my fire
Reach for the skies
In hopes to meet your own
they mix to form a cloud
To shadow my longing heart
And my fanning flames
I pray that it rains
To put this all out
And burry my pain in the ashes
Perhaps someday it will rise
In hopes of your love
And everything it brings me
A single touch
That takes my breath away
And give life back to me

~ A Dream

I'm dazzled by the belief that life is what may seem
I'm dazzled yet the most by my uninterpreted dreams
I'm dazzled to witness
All this unfinished business
But what dazzles me more
Those golden hearts settling for less and deserving more
It doesn't dazzle to compromise, give lovingly or sacrifice
What dazzles me when this is unappreciated or left unseen
For loved ones suffering in silence
Failed by expectations
That mankind is so generous
Generosity is not expenditure
Generosity is giving from a broken heart
For other ones to mend
I'm dazzled by the generosity of the skies
And the poverty here under
Can't wait to fly, cut loose these chain and wonder

~ Dazzled

My mentor, my muse, my mortifying mystic
My everyday mantra
My every night mourn
I've written a hundred and more poems
In your love
I can write a thousand more
Just a glimpse of you is all I need
To fill and fulfil my heart
What on earth is my crime
To send us worlds apart

~ On Longing

Shine on
Even if they escape your light
Shine on
It's their demons you fright
Shine on
If you blind them, it's not your fight
Shine on
Don't beware what you wish for
Shine on
Haven't you asked for this flight
Shine on
Haven't you known "I have more"

~ Listen to your Guides

Blindfolded, my heart sees
I follow your path
Before my eyes, doors opening to heaven
A sacred oath my heart honors
In full faith I step forward
Trusting you lead
Believing in you
blaming myself for my steeps
You are opening doors and closing them
As you please
Who am I to have a say
Or even question "why?"
If I'm obliged mischief
Your contentment is my relief
I surrender like leaves

~ Like Leaves

Trust the skies
Marvels are planned for your eyes
Trust the skies
Miracles are hardships in disguise
Trust the skies
Guide your heart if it denies
Haven't you been carried in the hands of fate
Has your Savior ever been late
Trust the skies
Mercy and misery intertwine
Love with all your heart and witness wonders
Don't bury yourself under your crumbles

~ Miracles Dwell in the Invisible

Beyond the sound of the crashing waves
There is a voice that I crave
A voice of wisdom, a voice of truth
A voice of tenderness wrapped in grace
Beyond the sound of the crashing waves
There is a voice with such embrace
Beyond the crowd
There is a wishful sound
Where all what feels like shelter bounds
Where all my armor shields fall down
Beyond the sound of the crashing waves there is a heart that aches
An eye that yearns to the depth you hold in your embrace
A hand that barely knows your touch
An eye that hardly sees your face
Behind the sound of the crashing waves
There's a soul longing beyond the seas
A depth of love greater than oceans
A heart that's worn on my sleeves
Offering masses of devotion

~ Beyond the Sound

All my deepest secrets
I've whispered to YOU in silence
A language non comprehendible
Except by true admirers
Who says that I am of mysteries
When I've confessed all that, I am and all that I am not
to YOU

~ Confession

You wish to lock me in a castle
And claim it heaven
We're destined to eternity
You lie to me
I have witnessed you hoping I was "she"
I speak of freedom and light and truth
You? Wealth and youth?
Where were you when my heart wept
Where were you when my womb bled
Where were you when I felt Ice cold lying next to you in bed
Now you wish to fix this mess?
Now you wish to handle this irreversible stress
Ask me not to forgive and forget
I love you
But I'll move on with no regrets
No plans will change me, no temptations shall alter
Who I'm meant to be
I'm a soul, wild, crazy and free
Cage me not, it shall never be

~ Free Hearted

The kindle in your eyes reminds me
It is your soul I know
Beyond whom you are
Beyond what you do
Your kindness captivates me
The words you pour whole heartedly
A scared light
magnet like
Has drawn me to you
What choice there is
Where lies Divinity

~ Divine

If my heart was not bound by a cage
It'd fly to YOU I'd circle around YOU
Twirl in ecstasy
Linger longer in the feeling
Setting me free
But it was made to bow in contentment
Teach me how to tame it instead
Teach me how to stand tall
Toe to head
Embrace gracefully all the longing
Never blame it
Oh dear lord
Let me be
Like a tree
Root me into the depth of earth
Fly my branches in heavens to eternity
Isn't Fire meant to put out every desire
But the one to be near YOU
Hasn't Abraham answered Gabriel
"From you I ask not"
I so long for the word of GOD
Was it his peace admitting fire
Here you burn every "other" desire
Here you do not long for another
What more to wish for
But to be with your LORD

~ Fire

A tale will someday be told
of how the skies showered
to camouflage her tears

~ No Coincidence

Here I am
Pouring my heart out at your feet
Not daring to look up to see
If you're looking down at me
So lift me up
Or let me be
Picking up the pieces of what's left of my dignity
I feel like a hundred years old
I've aged in your love
I've strived for heavens above
Now they seem more in my reach than you

~ Hopeless

They will keep failing you
blaming it on you
Until you realize it's not your fault
To be genuinely forgiving
And learn once and for all to forgive yourself
Forever believing in them

~ Mature

I'd hate you, like I'd smash out my bones
I'd love you, like I'd scatter my heart to stones
I'd miss you, like I'd miss my breath under water
I'd abandon you, like blood leaving my veins
I'd show you, if you'd let me
The power of this destiny
I'd tell you a tale every night
I won't lose a love battle
But I'd skip every fight
I'll witness miracles
And call them fate
I'll endure masses for your sake
I'll clean up everyone else's wound
I'll wash away everyone else's pain
I'll pray for the sun to rise
I'll plea for the sky to rain

~ Let It Rain

No I'm not falling back
In this trap of self-imprisonment
I've wept and bled too much
For these wings to spread

~ A Broken Angel

We grow older but not with years
With every lesson, every test
Every encounter with our fears
We grow older but not with time
With every hardship, every loss
Every betrayal of what's divine
We grow older but not in vain
With every failure of not being heard felt or seen
We grow older time after time
Aiming for finite pleasures
Striving for endless mirages
With empty souls and hungry hearts
Searching for mirrors in the unseen
We grow older but young reflections
Yet refuse to depart the young tales of our hearts

~ Young at Heart

Before your love I was lonely
With the whole world around
Before your love I was blind
Did not realize what I was missing out
Like when I saw you
I was found
Before your love I was ill
Did not learn what needed to heal
When people saw me, they were sorry
I learned to spare them their worry
Now that I have found love
Does it matter what I have lost
For they can only see the sorrow
But I can only hear the song

~ My Soul Song

You are the river
I am the stream
You are the calm night
I the ecstatic day
You are the moon
Enlightening my way
You are the treasure
I am the seeker
You are the healer
I am the wound
Whisper me those tales untold

~ You and I

Take me "there"
Where troubles end and souls sing
Where my heart grows wings
Where I escape the bitterness of hereunder
Where I roar my heart burdens like thunder
Where problems resolve and wars end
Where hypocrites get skinned of their pretend
Where hearts soften and souls grow
Where only the truth we're bound to know
Where light is night and day
And eternal rivers flow
Take me "there"
Where loved ones greet
and cheer each other in eternal retreat
Where no more worries are thought and no more heart aches are felt
Take me there on an infinite quest
Where the depth of YOUR knowledge is impossible to fetch
Take me "there"
My thirst is never quenched
For YOUR love I'll be thirsty
Far after "the end"

~ Inspired by an Angel

Don't ask me to longer stand
where I once stood
I'm a new one with each reviving breath
With every rising sun
With every new moon
I'm reborn
HIS will runs through me
How can I resist
Flooding rain and flowing streams
It's like asking a flower not to bloom
Change is inevitable
I'll Roll with it
Or else my soul shall perish

~ They Said You've Changed I Whispered 'I Wish'

It is equally essential to be loving
As to be loved
Or else
How will you discover
Your own depth
Spread your wings and fly ahead
What is holding you back are hinderance in your head
All this sky
All this space
Yet to choose to stay in your garnished cage
Reach for Grace in the clouds
Breath in Air
It's only fair
than to stay bound to earthly chains
Lose yourself in heavenly realms
Isn't it time you turn this page

~ Transformation

In the fields of YOUR love
My seeds are growing
Nourished by divine light
My secret calling
Guided by whom YOU love
It's where I'm falling
Into the well of YOUR knowledge
The truest calling

~ In Love We Don't Fall We Rise

Pouring off a fountain of a giant mountain
Water is love in pearls and glitters sprinkling
Showering us
What possibility there is to stop the force of gravity
Like stopping nature from being nature
Like banning a mother from giving nurture
What possibility there is
For a stream to stop its flow
This is what love feels about you

~ What Love Is

She is rebelling living between no longer and not yet
In HIS will she felt freed
Rejoicing the reflection of who she is
Learning that in her being
Right here Right now
She is mirroring HIM
Surrendering
Immersing in the secrets of the blue
Sofia how I wish to be you

~ One Moment in Time

Like leaves, we wilt, we fall
Like leaves we're born anew
Like leaves we gracefully let go
Why believe dead things grow
Like leaves we foresee past the fall
Have we learned just yet
Our hearts have seasons too

~ Seasons of the Heart

The healing waves that I embrace
Or just float among their crashes
I live and die
I burn to ashes
I dive in piles of thoughts
I wonder why
I thought "Can I"
It happens often
I trick myself to believe I'm almost home
I've reached my shore
What happens next an unexpected Guest to reassure "you can endure"
Of all life's lessons I'm sure there is one that will unfold this mystery
wash me in a healing ocean out of my misery
Allow me once more to rewrite my destiny

~ Not Yet Home

Darkness is here to show us
life's truest colors
we shed our layers
One after the other
until our essence embodies the light
only then we find the purpose of the quest
only then we learn the meaning of being
Only then we balance holding on and letting go
Only then we learn who we should turn to

~ Darkness Has a Role

It's not the threats that defeat us
It is more often than not
Our own vulnerability
You cannot hide from yourself
Go ahead try
Like an ostrich
Burry your head in the sand
Escape this land
Look away, hide your tears alter your tone
Where will you go
From the truth birthing in you
I promise… not far
You'll stumble in a mirror
Eventually
And What will it show
How long can you hide the real you

~ Self Talk

An avalanche of emotion
A sacred devotion
Steppingstones to paradise
A door to heaven
A soul on the rise
In discovering YOUR beauty
In the depth of YOUR oceans
I am willing to drawn deeper everyday
For my death is in reality a rebirth
Time after time

~ Rebirth

If I am to crush myself to fragments like the waves to the rocks
for YOUR sake I would
If I am to go back and forth like tides for YOUR sake I would
If I am to be still like quiescent water and wait
for YOUR sake I would
If I am to run like rivers and streams to merge in YOUR oceans
for YOUR sake I would
Ask me not what I would or would not do
I'd live and die a thousand times for YOU

~ On Adoration

Listen to the little voice
whispering from a distance
Reminding you "You have a choice!"
Courage has a sound
it says "Stand your ground"
Courage has a color resembling fire
Assuring that "You can"
embrace any plan
So long that you feel it
Beating with your heart

~ On Courage

She travels and comes back
Carrying on all the love she could hold in her heart from her journey to pass on the light to others
On her way home

~ A Giver

Bless the broken
Those whom life has failed a hundred times
they failed counting
Busy collecting their broken pieces
Bless the wounded
Who surrender to your wishes
Their prayer is to «JUST BE »
To only you and « IT IS »
Bless the kind
Who still have faith to trust
In those dull and drunken minds
Bless the caring
Who give heart and soul to others
What is love without sharing
Bless the blind
Who still believe despite the darkness
There's always way to your light
Bless the silent ones
They know what reaches you
Their words unspoken

~ Bless the Broken

Be the love you've once missed
Room the world free of wings
Conquer Souls and breach hearts
It was written in your stars
Mind no other but your truth
Honor the inner voice of yours
Tomorrow is a mystery so they say
Tomorrow will take your breath away

~ Believe

Every cell in my being calls for YOU
YOUR presence is healing in essence
I repent repeating YOUR name
My heart bares the blame
Save myself from imprisonment
Burry my burdens miles apart
I've suffered long from what I'm carrying
Is it time to mend my heart

~ On Healing

When I leave
Do not weep
For I'd finally be with the beloved
A long waited for encounter
Should be ceremonial
I've passed this door
A thousand times and more
Lived and died as many
Pleading HIS contentment
Let me go now
My wings are ready

~ When Wings Are Ready

I'm no angel
Can you see my wings
Perhaps you're deceived
By the softness I speak
I'm no angel
May be I travel spaces
My soul roams different Places
But I'm no angel
Perhaps I'm keen with others who're mean
But I'm no angel
I have fears
Of separation, letting go
And expectations
I feel abandoned
When I can't feel you
I get frustrated and fragile
And yet say I'm fine
I'm no angel
I endure and endure
While cracking on the inside
I'm no angel

~ I'm No Angel

A calling for a mountain's embrace
A whisper from YOUR grace
One step at a time on the journey to the wisdom of YOUR knowing
One more chance to see YOUR face

~ One Chance

I want to flood the world with love
Witness waterfalls fill kindled hearts
Drown in oceans of dreams and silhouettes
Set doubts worlds apart
Ignite sorrows to blown ashes
Stream rivers in broken hearts

~ A Lover's Dream

I've seen a castle in the darkness of the night
The moon in its brightest light
Angel wings flying over my head
So many I've lost count
I've seen a tree with blooming flowers disappearing replaced by a full moon
In a blue-sky realm
I've seen waves of turbulence
Roaring lions and vicious snakes
And settled souls that do not shake
I've seen signs, messages
I've heard voices of the truth
How can my humble soul contain this beauty
Face adversity with a dress of grace
Without your light I'll get lost
In your light I shall be found
Lead me, guide me, take my hand
Fetch my heart and clear my soul
Look at me
I shall see more

~ The Eyes of the Heart

Her mystic friend said
Read your book
Something grand is going to happen next
She threw it halfway on the shelf
Afraid she'd face the truth
Too scared of standing for herself
Then HIS light shone down on her
She felt serene, content and free
Did not hope for anything more
She has been going around in circles
Searching for the truth
Surpassing the fact that all she needed to do
Was go read her book

~ The Truth Lies Within

Do you know what air does to earth, it forms storms
Do you know what air does to fire, if fans the flames
Do you know what air does to water, it ripples waves
Do not underestimate what you do not see
While the unseen resides in the seen
Do you recognize the air in me

~ Says the wind

All this insight and you pretend to not see
The truth I bare is killing me
Wish not the unfaithful to be free
Maybe they long for their cages more than to roam HIS skies
or swim HIS seas
let them BE
What about me
Shed this false skin off me
I'm tortured by pretending
Set me free

~ A Plea

Unfold the secrets of YOUR creation
What's the spell of this magic potion
The kind of love that make seeds grow and flowers bloom
That makes leaves shed in fall yet grateful to the trees
That makes a mother bend and kneel for her children's embrace
stay awake all night with no complains with full hearts faith
That makes streams flow to rivers and rivers to seas
That makes people foresee the truth of this reality
That binds souls in nods of love despite of the time they spend apart
That makes love flow despite the distance between the shadows of their hearts
That brings contentment in a silent prayer
And makes forgiveness dwell in the midst of the scars of our hearts
That makes us secretly accept exactly where we are
Teach me your secrets I strive to know
All this love described is YOU

~ Sacred Contemplation

I love you for all the blood once shed
I'll love you till the rise of the dead
I love you for all the days gone by
I'll love you no space for goodbyes
I love you so long the night is dark
I'll love you till our souls embark

~ I'll Always Love You

Call me nuts
Call me crazy
Call me mad
Call me names neither you
Or me will understand
So long I am in love with all what exists
So long as I dance to the tunes of the universe
So long as I hear the rhythms of these beating hearts
So long as my heart still sings to the ones who part
I embrace the lunacy for my part
May this mania never depart my heart

~ Embracing Madness

Some wish to rape your soul
Others presume you're whole
But the ones who see you wholeheartedly
Are the ones worth fighting for

~ Choose Your Battles Wisely

What if I forget
Will you remind me
Of the racing thoughts that used
To crumble inside my head
What if I forget
The names of the faces that added meaning to my life instead
What if I forget
The love that kept me going
The recipe that keeps life flowing
What if I forget the kindest words and the Harshest ones
That shaped my lessons and vanished undone
What if I forget
The ring of your voice
When my nights were dark
I had no choice but to flee apart
Not knowing that escaping you is in reality
Escaping my reality
Not learning that I'll be fighting myself Instead

~ What if I Forget

Isn't it satisfying to know
The laws of the universe
Will reunite our atoms the way we were before creation
Like Adam and Eve
Is it enough to confide
That you and I will be One once more
Isn't safe to believe
We'll be home

~ *Reunion*

I lost my all
To find myself
It turned out vital
For the mystery of the journey to reveal itself
Why act small
When the whole universe lies within thy self

~ Losing Yourself Is Not a Waste of Time

Can you only imagine the wildflowers
Growing in my heart
The colorful scenery I'm witnessing beyond worlds apart
Do you smell the dew after the rain
Will you swear my love is not in vain
Will you dance in the wind and sing my song
Will you hold my heart for so long
Will you dare to be true
With all what it takes of you
Can you hear the lingering chants of the hummingbirds
Will you ask them why they deserted my land
Can you chase the sun and call for the moon
Will you pray night and day we become whole
Did you answer the call from that far away land
Does my heart understand what I'm meant to understand
Will the colors of the rainbow shade our years
Will the shadows of our realities disappear
Will you be my moon
And I your sun
Will you remember me long after I'm gone

~ Will You Love Me This Much

Even the rules of languages
Break for Poetry's sake

~ We Learn Rules to Break Them

Make me a bush in YOUR desert
Make me one of YOUR seeds
Make me a soldier who moves where YOU
please, how you please
Make me fish in YOUR seas
A Bird that roams YOUR skies
Make me a serpent that carries poison but do not die
Make me an awl that goes to sleep by sunrise
Make me a shark that goes hunting blind at night
Make me whatever you make of me
For THEE
I'll totally BE

~ On Being

And when I'm gone
I will confess
I was once loved
My heart was touched by the hands of GOD
I was once known
I was once seen
I was once heard
With not one interpreted word

~ I Was Once Loved

How do you leash him when he's young and wild and free
How do you tell him "I understand you ache for freedom"
How do you keep him when your nest he needs to flee
How'd he know It's your heart you're suddenly stepping on
Bless his steps with your bleeding heart
Cherish every single moment in his life from the start
Guide him now for Tomorrow
is not yours to borrow
Tell him Son you are now a Man
Trust your soul
And it shall guide you home

~ Your Children Are Earth's Seeds They too Long to Grow

I'm no sin
No crime no felony
Run away for a hundred years
Hide under your thousand shields
Drown in your auspicious guilt
No one escapes their destiny

~ Destined No Sin

In the isles, mountains and valleys of your being
You shall rise and fall
You shall hear HIS call
You shall moan and cry and howl
You shall whisper in your depth
But the echoes won't settle for less
It shall rise in passion
To the Seventh heaven
So your soul can rest

~ Serenity at Its Best

Water is soft but it carves stone
A subtle flow does pave streams
penetrate caves and shape dreams
Water is transparent like clear hearts
So long for the thirsty
Whom has known love in transparency
drinking the elixir to revive their lives
Pouring out their souls to mend others and themselves
We're made of water, you know?
May we outpour, shed, stream and flow

~ A lot Like Water

If you are to love me
Then love my cracks my flaws and all else
That is not as I may seem
If you are to love me
walk along with me as I heal
If you are to love me
Then your love do not conceal
A love so true
Sheds guards off you
Softens you
Who claimed, "Love hard?"
When only what's yielding
steals hearts
If you are to love me
Be you and let me Be
Unapologetically
A love so true
Sheds layers off you
a love so true
Blows life into you

~ To Love of the Broken Pieces

I've been unheard
Unseen, unfelt
Only YOU have mirrored my strength

~ I Now Know Love

I'm not a toy in your hands
I'm not the maiden of your dreams
She wanted to run out and scream
But then her heart breaks
Whispers in aches
"But he never promised you anything"

~ Never Promised

Of all the chances I've been given
The moments worth living
I cherish the ones I'm close to YOU
The breath in my bones
That carves life out of mud and stone
In the softness of YOUR encounter
What's worth is life without surrender
With all my heart and soul I call
"ALLAH" my savior
Let loose my chains so I see you
Freed like a bird not wearing wings
My all is bare carrying my sins
I reach for you
I give in

~ Worship

There is no opposite to LOVE
LOVE is all there is
"I hate you" is a cry
"It hurts to love this much"
What can replace love
Ask not my heart
It does not know
Love cannot be replaced
Love leaves no room
For darkness to grow
Love does not end
It fades away like a dying sun
Rising in different earthly parts
Replacing cold hearts with warmer hearts
Love lives decades and decades
In utterly faithful hearts

~ Love Is All There Is

With each fluffing letter
Of every passing poem
My hearts lives anew
What worth are my words
If they cannot reach you

~ Revived

Both feet on the ground
But the soul not bound
I roam around heavens
The skies till seventh
So I would reach home
Yearning for the truth
Buried beyond layers
Of a hundred false selves
Reaching out for YOU
Through this ancient battle
To conquer myself
Shelter me here with YOU
Save me from myself

~ Clarity

What language do I need
When you can hear my silence speak
I tremble from this knowing
The freedom I feel
Having no voice
Beyond worldly telling
What pleas have I chased
Having no choice
My choice is mere flowing
With you all steps are blissful
No moves
I'm carried

~ The Hands of God

You spare me moments of Eden
For your presence I am as thirsty as ever
I wish to uncover everything about you
All the details of your being
your tiny memories, your victories, your likes, dislikes
and all in between
what you regard sacred
what you regard mean
I want to be closer to you than the air you inhale to your chest
I want to smell the warmth of the softness of your breath
Tingle and shiver from your touch
Dance in heaven in your embrace
What can I fear to face
If you're the one by my side
if I were not the woman I am today
I wouldn't have learned to love likewise.

~ Eden

Is the évitable or inevitable
What leaves us broken

~ A Quest

I'd escape in caves to love you
I'd climb mountains and dive in seas to love you
I'd run miles and miles
To love you
I'd live and die a thousand times
To love you
I'd switch lives and swear to fly
To love you
I'd work so hard bare sleepless nights
To love you
I'd shatter apart, break my own heart
To Love you
I'd serve your purpose for years and years
What more can I do
To prove my love to you

~ To Love You

What more to love the tiny footprints of my baby's feet
The chill of the morning breeze
The gentle words that my heart breach
What more to love
The dawn's singing birds
the nightingales
The fluff of my eternally loyal dogs
my friend's secret tales
What more to love
The strikes of the waves on the rocks
The storms that shake our hearts out
What more to love
The smiles behind the spilled tears
The patience that streamed our years
The promise of tomorrows
To wash our past sorrows
What more to love
The ink spilling of my pen like blood from the crusade of sacrifice
The mastering of hiding the truth
And wearing in pride the disguise
What more to love
The grace in adversity
Or the surrender and vulnerability in love
The solitude that pours down your light on us
What more to love
Than your heavens above

~ *What More to Love*

Pardon a poet
Words come running like waves rebelling
Stillness
Dying for recognition
To the ones thirsty for their sips
Don't you know yet
Words have a taste

~ Rebellious

Heaven's gates
Are eight
Open wide for the ones who know
It's never late to go knock on heavens gates
All the roads lead to Rome
The ancient said
How about souls who roam
A hundred paths to meet their fate
Or those aching hearts who wait
For their loved ones by heaven's gate

~ Heaven's Gate

Silence transcends speech
Feelings transcend thoughts
Meanings transcend feelings
Being transcends meanings
How far can we reach
Where shall we stop
Every step is a move towards a safer haven
Choose your battles wise one
Not all are worth fighting

~ *Transcendence*

They taught us love is blind
They lied
Only love has eyes
So close as the sun in the early morning rays
So close as the moon in the darkest shades of dawn
Like day and night
We are
Like a thousand miles apart
I seize to look for you my love
I find you in my heart

~ So Close

What if I appear
In your space and disappear
In the shadow of this world
to be contained in your soulful embrace
What if this life is the illusion
And the reality is in the realm of space
What if I let go of the density of the material world
And submerge in the light of your face
What if I manifest my story
with the mighty powers given by "HU"
What if I deny all the voices who cry NO
What if I honored the forgotten oath
And get drawn only to YOU

~ The Sacred Call

The tip of the iceberg
On the surface of the water
Is the part that shows of my love
Above… the Ice
Beneath… the fire
The Duality of YOUR creation
surpassing desire
The seas and oceans cannot witness enough
The realms, the visions, the heavens above
Can no longer bare more of this blazing love
If I am to draw my love
I'll draw an iceberg

~ Truth Resembles an Iceberg

Who am I to fool
My heart follows no book, no rule
Driven by wings of fire
Freedom is my module
Roam along with me
The sky is my referee

~ On Freedom

Meeting as strangers in the facade of life
But One in essence
Before the making of time
Unity then it is
The branches of a tree belonging
the stems rooting
The leaves rising in heaven
Holding on against the winds of change
Utterly Familiar then
Long after years of renegade

~ Unity

Where do I go
When everywhere I'm reminded of you
How do I leave
When you taught me everything I've achieved
How can I stray
When my heart will not lead me astray
Where do I escape
When my heart I cannot escape
Where can I hide
When there is no where you can't find me

~ You Can Run Not Hide

I would drown you in love it would be difficult to catch your breath
I'll flood you with poems you'd go speechless
I'll paint your dreams and turn them to realities
I'll have your back in adversities
I'd fly to you; you'd wish you'd chain my heart
I cherish every memory that united us
Even the streets I roamed thinking of you
Every step I take is a wish to get me closer
Passing by the words you once read or hearing a word you once said
Meeting anyone who knows you
Is yet seeing you instead
Every sound that resembles your voice
Every word that sounds like you
Every beautiful view
I tend in my heart to share with you
I cherish your wisdom in every wise man's speech
I find your words in the little words I preach
I cherish you in the feelings I feel
I swear to myself they were real
Is it possible to deny you're in everything I do

~ Gone Not Forgotten

Two souls intertwined
Living their lives in parallel
Timelines
Crossing paths every time
Like an infinity sign

~ Souls Are Made in Pairs

I'd move mountains by YOUR mighty strength
I'd chase my fears they'd disappear
I'd climb up hills
Dig down mines
I'll flood the world with Poems
And claim them mine
I'd rise and fall in my ruins
As long as I'm transcending
This spiral path is never ending
I call for your hand, I'm not pretending

~ My Call Is Real

I sank in your blue
With feelings so true
Now that I've found you
Will you ever let me go

~ Drowning

How do you feel when love surrounds
Accepted
Contained Fulfilled
Or filled with divine presence
One can never compare with what else feels
How do you feel when you're in circles of truth
Freed like a bird
Appreciate where you stand
Where is this truth
Fly me to their land
How will you feel when this all ends
Content
Or will you dwell on the scattered pieces
You've shared with them
And their pieces they've shared with you
Free or will you dwell
"where are the pieces I've left behind of me?"
How will you know you have found the truth
Trust me you will know
And if you don't the truth will find you

~ A Seeker

Forever your name
I'll hum

~ Mantra

This silver hair
In the mirror
catching my stare
Is becoming precious
It carries the color of the moments
I once dared
The fears I did not share
My flares, my like thunder inner blares
My sadness, my sorrow
My inner child longing
The silver lining
Reminding
To this world
We're not belonging

~ The Silver Lining

Every step I take towards your depth
Fills my spirit with inexplicable strength
Your blue has mirrored my own
Be it color
Be it being
Be it tone

~ The Blue

What do I have to sacrifice
To attain YOUR closeness

I give up my will in delight
To the will of YOUR Greatness

I no longer need to fight
To drown in flooding light

Every day is a fête
So long as I'm by YOUR gate

Knock knock I pray
"Please let me stay"

~A Prayer

YOU have created us in pairs
And made our souls to settle and care
How did we abandon YOUR grace
And towards our egos we stared
Startle our hearts with secrets
Who said we cannot experience
YOUR heaven here under

~Haven vs Heaven

A loner, you are
You chose to watch from afar
Minding not who comes, who goes
Minding yet to choose what HE is to choose
A loner, you are
Staying close no matter how far
where the light resides
You tend to fantasize
Drawing magic from a distant star
A loner you are

~ A Loner

It is alluring that no words are there to describe
What leaves us speechless

~ Speechless

Until when you'll regard me as Sin
When will your heart give in
My flowing rivers are not enough
To flood your streams?
My growing heart isn't big enough to drown your fears
My soul is not passionate enough to reach higher than you aspire
Am I drawn to you by earthly desires
How many times do I have to slay myself
To stay close to you

~ Desperate

Like a feather in the wind
Like a loose end
Fly me where YOU wish
I trust where the winds take me
YOUR tunes are the melody of destiny
How doubt, it's YOUR play
Do actors have a say

~ YOUR Wish Is My Desire

I drown in the oceans of your eyes and dive
For many years I've known death
Now I've experienced to feel alive
I'm drawn to all the possibilities of being
I've long denied the gift of foreseeing
Kill me and revive me a hundred times
As long as my heart returns to you

~ Repentance

Withdrawn
An act so quite
A cry so loud

~ Withdrawn

Unique you are "Says your name"
The fragrance of your words to the light of the throne pertains
Flooding hearts with love's wisdom
In its purest form
Master what have you witnessed?
Your words magnificent tales
Take my hand
From sky to sky
From door to door
Thirsty to explore what you have explored
"The conference of the birds"
Of a faraway land where souls understand what minds withstand
Take my hand

~ A Letter Sent Through Time

Do not listen to yourself when it separates you from me
There is a knowing a soul bares
A blessing that is rare
That brings together
Those hearts of feathers
In a union so true
So does it matter if you were I
Or I was you
A mystery of the mysteries
The ONE will unfold for you

~ One

If all of life I'm bound to lose
In my heart
It's YOU I choose

~ A Choice

The greatest of battles is
Between the heart and the mind
In their balance lies great insight
Fight your heart and it shall ruin you
Follow your mind it shall enslave
Trust your spirit
From your ruins it shall save you
In the darkness of the fight
There is light towards great sight
Even If you are blinded by thee
HIS striking light will set you free

~ Set Free

Pondering in the thoughts of blue
Halting my heart away from you
Drifting apart from realities separating us
In the magnificence of the blue
My soul caressing you in mercy
Are we together in this journey
Do you feel me reaching for you
Can you see the depth of the well
I've thrown my heart into
It is your love manifested through
So teach me now what I should do
To keep myself away from you

~ A Truth I Can't Escape

Where do I hide
From inspiration like tide
Where do I go
From thoughts like waves of you

~ Inspiration

Full moon and the blue
Miles of ripple thoughts of YOU
All the beauty YOU made
in the depth of my heart engraved
Shimmering lights on this bay
Stills the rhythm of my breath
Come what may
So long as YOU fill my soul
With colors of a rainbow
Just a walk on YOUR shore
Fades my fears YOU reassure
All the secrets between US
GOD my heart longs for MORE

~ Reassured

She stared at the blue
And swore "I'm true"
Let me love, let me live
Let me dive into you
She asked for more
The blue laughed "Girl, beware what you wish for"
You are not here to fly up high
You will have to go through my storms, my tides, my crashes, my whirlpools, my roars
She nodded "Sure"
All what you wish for I'll endure
Where shall I go with this fire
How do I pursue my heart's desires
Who do I turn to except to you
The blue smiled "Here you go"
She lived and loved and dived and drowned time after time after time after time
That's the story of Sofia and her secrets of the blue

~ Secrets of the Blue

If madness is key
I'd sell my soul for free
And dwell by YOUR door
In hope to eternity

~ Fair Bargain

If I am to surf these waves
Then let me drown
I've fought for long
I'm tired of this struggle
Drown me
Or let the waves carry me
Where I belong
I surrender to the mighty will
Of the waters

~ Tired

I am a traveler
To a faraway land
My destination is of no end
In eternal passion my soul shall mend
But the journey here is weary
Where all else fades but YOU
All the feelings are ineffable
The flames turn into ashes
All willingly for YOU
To warm the heart with certainty
In the beginning
I was with YOU
And eventually I'll end with YOU

~ Someone Called Home

You have abandoned me
Once every while I believe
in your presence
Needless to say
Needless to be
You have abandoned me
Minor flames we shared birthing together wildfires burning
within me
You have abandoned me
A spark in the dark
To a soul stark
slaying myself
Igniting fire out of desire
To stay close to you
And what else you do
You still abandon me

~Abandoned

A message in a bottle
Thrown into the sea
Whispering if I had a wish
It would be that YOU find me
For I'd lose myself in the search of YOU
Ain't this why YOU put me through
What YOU put me through
So what a win if I lost all of me to find YOU
And what a loss if I return with everything but YOU
It matters not the most who will find who
They said long ago
What you seek is seeking you

~ Message in a Bottle

What is a star
Twinkling in the dark
eternally patient
Waiting you are
What is a star
Shining on forever
Do you need approval
To be who you are
What is star
Forming constellations
Vivid manifestations
Constant affirmation
Determining who you are
What is a star
Burning since forever
Lighting for another
Have you seen your beauty
Being what you are
What is a star

~ What Is a Star

You keep going around in circles
To reach the truth in disguise
At times diving deep in water so quite
Other times rushing like wildfire
Can't withhold your soul's desire
Keep going thirsty one
The spiral path is of no end
An eternal mystery
An infinite possibility
Promising your heart growth
Beyond your minds ability

~ Keep Going

The past is gone
The future not known
Be present it is a "win win"
No pain, no gain
And all is one

~ Here and Now

How I wish to see his face even in a dream for now
How I long to feel his touch
Even in the realms for now
How I wish to hear his voice
Even in my imagination
One gaze gives life to a heart
Revives all Sensation
Mercy on this aching heart
Longing for salvation

~ Seeking Salvation

I'm drowning I'm falling
I hear your heart calling
No depths of seas
No mountain's breeze
No highs or lows
Can just increase this pitch of love
Screaming through skies above
echoing my love

~ Echo

Befriend your heart
It beats for you moment in
Moment out
It calls for your existence
Its well-being too
Depends on you
Befriend your heart
Stop tearing it apart
Watching everything they do
Believe what it calls for is true
Befriend your heart
Haven't you carried it all along
How many times you had it broken
The heartache, the disappointments,
The confusion, the overwhelms.
Has it ever failed you
Be friend your heart
Until the very end, my friend
It keeps beating for you

~ Befriend Your Heart

Just you and I and this moment
No past, no future
Harmony that feels eternal
A pure form of bliss
Like everything seize to exist
If only I can capture the power of my own breath
Feel more of blessings and worry less
If only I can freeze this feeling of divine closeness and recall
it every time I need strength
Teach me how this suffering ends

~ A Precious Lesson

We think it's love
When it makes us whirl and twirl
When we go head over heals
When our heads spin and our hearts skip a beat
When butterflies ruffle our stomachs
We think it's love and it turns to be a lesson
Love changes course
Love comes around in a hundred different ways and forms
Love does not just allow you to dream and fly
Love grounds you, surrounds you
Love gives you a true taste of life
Love revives you
Love warms your heart
Love enlightens you
Who are we to dictate love on how we want our lives to flow
For it is HIS pen and HE writes glory
We're just scripts in a Great writer's hand
A great love's vision that will out stand
Will move mountains, cross valleys and stretch skies
so far beyond where we now stand
We're just puppets in Great God's hands

~ A Greater Vision

Often do I dream
of a predetermined destiny
an intertwine of souls
a blessing, a curse?
a non-conventional destination
a route I'm obliged to take
a path
or a pass
a door to a sacred space
a symphony of angelic tunes
a fight with sheer blasphemy
a love of no explanation
a spiral transcendental rhapsody

~ Entanglement

A constellation of a vivid
artistic Imagination
In the balance of the scale
of emotions and her brain
Comes all else
Swaying in between
What is seen and what is unseen
Drawn into a mystic reality
Leaving parts and particles beyond
In hopes to see in clarity
What should and should not be done
What an undeniable truth
In a bonfire of her youth
Let her burn into ashes
in her rise
she'll rise in ruth

~ Libra

Perhaps it's time
But you don't know just yet
Tables are turned in a moment I bet
Perhaps it's now
What you seek in tomorrow
is already ours why dwell in sorrow
Perhaps it's past
What we dread to last
Perhaps it's done
What we thought was none
All the fears surpass
What we feel would last
All the love we share
Have no match but "there"
Perhaps it's near
and will suddenly appear
Do you know my love
What I hold so dear?
It's the knowing I cherish
That you're forever here

~ An Illusion Called Time

The whistling winds
The screaming thunder
The traveling clouds that blend encounters
The bells of prayers,
the chants
the hums
The deserts of sands
The blues of oceans
The vast lands
A lantern of light
shining through the darkest of nights
The songs of angels
The hustles of devils
What's felt unsaid
What's left undone
The rise of the dead
All call for the ONE

~ The Sacred Call

The more I surrender
The more I fall
The more I strive
The more I dive
In the core of love
Is there an answer to this call
Between the push and pull
I hardly survive

I see Colors of Eden
Like northern lights
Into their green I'm drawn without a fight
In a simple step
My soul takes flight
To the grace of your face
An unmatched paradise

~ I Have Seen GOD

Burn
Burn in shelter, in escape, in refuge
Burn in a sacred secret space of destiny
Burn in shame or in contentment
Burn in ecstasy
Burn in sweetness or in endeavors
Of sacrifice
Burn layers of ego, shadows, traumas and hidden vice
Burn the falsehood of your earthly fights
Burn your depths to screams and aches
Burn your flames and ashes will light the way for others to find
Burn my love
Burn in Delight

~ Light and Fire

May we indulge in trees with stems of words
branches in alphabets
and Fruits of dangling letters
Like hummingbirds
May we birth poems no one has ever heard and pitch out melodies to quench the thirst in heavenly rhymes
May we spill lyrics for angels to sip and eternally sing
May we drawn in light
Rise above all other things

~ Poets Prayers

You willing to talk
One word feels like a long walk
perhaps it's our dreams in the night we stalk
Your voice is music to my ears
A note that is sincere
One sweeps away my fears
One is a promise "I'm forever near"
Your silence is lavish
In its grace I vanish
I disappear

~ Silence too Has a Voice

Halt my heart
Halt my soul
Halt my fingers
My pen will recall
what is banned by the mind
In the fire
The ashes will carry the depths of desire
Halt the words
Halt the meanings in my silence I'm concealing
In the darkness of the night
It's myself I'm forged to fight
Will they ever see the light
Or forever hide in feelings

~ The Battle

She is with us
We are separate but one in essence
like the branches of a tree many
But together
Can you see them belong
Swaying along in heaven
Their stem so strong
Dreaming of the day
breathing in the light
Sipping in the soul of earth
Bathing in the warmth of the sun
They are one

~ Faithful

Ask me not to endure
My heart is aching with no cure
Ask my soul not to withstand
no greater pain than one banished from their land
Ask me not my mission fulfill
In this longing I'm falling ill

~ Sick of Longing

We interpret meanings of uttered words
Why choose to deny what is meant and believe
what's heard
Why not listen to what is felt instead
Why not immerse in Life toe to head
Know that lessons shall repeat themselves until we break the
pattern
A compass hidden in our hearts
An inner lantern
Fight or flight
Drawn or float
Choices we make every moment shape us, make us break us
or direct us to divine presence
Which road to follow
A direct path or a deceptive hollow
We seek until we find
A never-ending spiral light

~ A Spiral Path

I defend you
In my utmost fragility
I defend you
Through the walls you build I see
the fields behind your shields
The softness of the core
Beyond your hard shell
How do I know you so well?

~ Inner Knowing

I once thought love was an explosion
A bomb of infatuation
An accumulation of emotion
A long-term captivation
Until I learned what love is not
Love is a secret
a giving rain
a flowing stream
Love is no ordinary mundane dream
Love is a never-ending longing
Swept solely by pretending
So I believed one once said
You can't know what love is
Until you learn what love is not

~ What Is Not Love

I was wondering if the color of heaven was blue
And if not so
What colors would there be
The green hiding behind the eyes of those who see
The white resembling the light in their hearts
What color is grace in adversity
What color is my longing to YOU
Is heaven the color of the rainbow
Or heaven is One look at YOU

~ Prism

It is hazardous to love
as it is reckless not to
Like stepping into an ocean
You have to walk with caution
The waves awaiting
but so are the treasures
I wish to be freed from YOUR love
If I wish to lose my sight and senses

~ *Never*

In a blissful moment of unity
When the heart was swept to eternity
and The soul not bound by what's earthy
The moon was shining in entirety
She who had nothing to hide
Drowning in oceans
All seeing
Standing bare before all tides
She suddenly Felt sorry for a world
Walking amid chaos blind

~ Awakened

Do you love my soul
Or do You love me whole
My flaws
My falls
My Perusing my call
My thrive to strive till the end
Or only my heart shall I befriend

~ Alone

I'm not this pain
I'm distant from this hurricane
I'll rise above the highest mountain
Until I reach the light
My soul I will maintain
I'll not fight for what's mundane
I care less
Myself I won't explain
I'll break this chain

~ Pattern

What is it with Sunsets and I
Is it the dying of the day
Or the hope of a glowing ray
Is it the ending and a new beginning or just the relish in silver linings
Is it the promise of a full moon
Or till the end of time it's doom
Is she content about it all
Will she forever stand this tall
Or for her to witness the night
She'll still have to shine so bright

~ Sun

Perhaps we're meant to cross each other's paths
Perhaps what we think would last won't last
Some people are milestones
Others just a flash
In a life but a dream
An illusion would ever last?
A mystic reality
Let the past just pass
In room for tomorrow
Let your light surpass
On a journey of self-discovery
What option is there to bypass

~ Never Lasting

To love is to await no validation
An open-ended contemplation
fair enough from your side when you witness the light
To love is to BE
No expectations
Minding not if others shine or if their spark subsides
so long as you follow the light
To love is non compared to infatuation
But how can you tell the difference if in your heart
Other than light resides
To love is to care no more of positions, status or belongings
Go ruin your reputation
Care no more of presentation or fake shows of manifestations
If your soul has matched your tribe
To love is indifference, submission
Resignation
To love is a mystery in our modern time

~ Definition

Little thoughts
Little goals
Little beams
Little steps pave your dreams

~ One Step a Time

Love yourself enough to find true love
Lead a journey to thy self
No analogy no rational no mental state can do it for you
Only the heart can carry you through
Dive into your soul
Remember what life has made you forget
Move on with no regrets
It is fine to need small gestures, smiles, kind words or a gentle touch or else why were made to feel so much
Yet no one is bound to suffer
The treasures of the ONE awaits in your heart but dear who implied
You're ever apart
I AM just a thought away from you
A breath of life in a single word of his is mighty enough to revive you
'Call for me
I'm ever here'
God is the savior my dear

~ The Healer

I ever wonder how many versions of myself I've left behind
I wonder evermore how many of myself I failed to find
I wonder why this quest is forever in my heart and on my mind
A journey embarked with no destination but merely ONE to find
With a path so treasured
So purifying
So long
I wonder if my soul at the end I'll recognize

~ Evolving

I had a message from the sky
For you and I
In the midst of a day covered in grey
When all seemed dull
A play misplayed
There was a heart shaped cloud
Followed by showers of rain
"You're loved by heavens"
lose your frown
The only constant is change!
Another day will come
When it rains
a sunny day
Never doubt the skies
All secrets prevailed

~ Raining a Promise

Think of all the poems I wrote
In honor of your love
Hundreds of them
Thousands of words inspired by you
Imagine the ones I never had the chance to write too
The ones I uttered before I fell asleep
The ones that ran in my mind as I dived in water so deep
The racing thoughts in my long walks
or as I fell in child pose
The ones I plead in prayer
The foggy ones in my daydreams
All that should have flooded my papers like streams and evaporated instead
the ones suffocated in stubbornness inside my head
Imagine the arguments I had with you
The ones I screamed how dare you?!
the conversations that were so smooth ending with a whisper
"I love you"
Imagine a world where silence had a voice and hearts of their choice
If I'm to create a version of Adam and Eve all true
I'd imagine a world of mine revolving around you

~ All True

YOU are salvation to me
I see YOU in all the faces
I hear YOU in every melody
I smell YOU in every breeze
All the gazes that are deep
All the silence
All the stillness
Filled with YOUR presence
How is love so captivating
With chains unseen
And screams unheard
With aches and mourns that toss and turn
With hopes that are not met
Thousands of words unsaid
encounters delayed
and Dreams unfulfilled
And though in a scale of eternity
This life is but a day or two
With a heart filled with YOU
I plea
YOU are salvation to me

~ Salvation

Never have you GOD given me
What I deeply wished for
Like YOU were guarding my heart
From need
From failures
From ailments that a heart is doomed to touch
YOU have made hearts bound to rush too much
But then YOU give more than I ever longed for
You blow away my soul
The KING of the Kings YOU are for sure
I know now GOD to let go is the lesson
I bow by your door
surrender with all my might
Immersed in rivers of gratitude to the oceans of
YOUR miracles I'm secretly tied
I'm bathing in YOUR light
My purpose I will find

~ Grateful

*Setting like an angel into the
depth of the sea
Wondering if water is to extinguish the fire within me
Aiming to dive till I cannot catch my breath
For the shallow is not meant for me
They call me sun
But am I the one
The only
Does their world truly whirl around me
Or am I too, blinded by the light
Is it the ocean
Or am I drowning in the gaze of their heavenly sight
I am melting down my blaze
In an ocean of utter devotion
Just because HE has chosen
It's time to sway out of sight
Can't ask why I should
seemingly die
when I was only born to shine*

~ Setting in an Ocean

Let heaven & earth celebrate us
Let rivers flow
Let birds flutter their wings
Let Angels Move around on rings
Let our tribe dance to the rhythms of our hearts
Ask the sun to shine
Ask the moon seize to die
Let thunder roar with love
Let volcanoes fire in passion
Ask oceans to stop their tides
Ask deserts to blossom
Pave the path with possibilities against all odds for your lovers
Let angels put down their wings
I am witnessing heavens sing

~ Presence